WARNING: This book contains str
language and profanity including e

A

Activis
noun
1. lean, drank

EXAMPLE: "I only sip Actavis 'cause it's my medicine"

act up
phrase

acting up is a way to foreshadow something someone wants to do to you; similar to "getting you going" or "in the mood".

EXAMPLE: "ooh baby, you look good in that outfit; you finna make me act up"

B

bag
noun
1. money

EXAMPLE: "I'm going to go get the bag

bando
noun
1. an abandoned house, a trap house

EXAMPLE: "Fill the bando up with bags

Barbz or Barbies
noun
1. Nicki Minaj's fan base

EXAMPLE: "Yeah, my money's so tall that my Barbies got to climb it/Hotter than a Middle Eastern climate, violent"—Nicki Minaj on Kanye West's "Monster"

Bet

Its like saying: Yes, ok, "it's on."

Big mad

Term used to describe when someone is excessively angry.

EXAMPLE: "Oooo she big mad?"

Bugging

to freak out or be upset
The same as tripping
EXAMPLE: "Why you bugging man? I told you I'd return your cd's."

bussin'
adjective
1. to let gun shots ring out
2. something that is very good

EXAMPLE: "This is bussin"

cake
noun
1. a big butt
2. money

EXAMPLE: "Dam she got cake"

cap
noun
1. lying
2. the top of one's head
3. to take one's head off

EXAMPLE: "you went out with about 80 women that is cap bro"

chicken
noun
1. money

EXAMPLE: "I be gettin' to the chicken, countin' to the chicken/And all of my n@$%#s gon' split it"—Desiigner's "Panda"

crack
adjective
1. something really good and addicting

EXAMPLE: "She was snorting crack yesterday bro"

D

dab
noun
1. dance move

EXAMPLE: "Hit the dab"

dat way
phrase
1. For real
2. To curve or swerve in a certain direction

EXAMPLE: "N@$%# try Lil' Tay-K, it's gon' be his last day/If you not talkin' 'bout smoke, you could go dat way"—Tay-K's "Dat Way"

deadass
adverb
1. seriously

EXAMPLE: "Are you deadass"

don
noun
1. A boss, the head of crew

EXAMPLE: "When you the don, you understand and you oversee it"—Big Sean's "Offense" featuring Babyface Ray and 42 Dugg

drip
adjective
1. a cool outfit

EXAMPLE: "Keep my head above the water while I drown in wealth/I got that drip like Gunna, I may drip or drown myself"—Juice Wrld's "Stay High"

drill
verb
1. to kill someone, something

EXAMPLE: "The type of shit'll make me flip out and just kill somethin'/Drill somethin', get ill and fill ratchets with a lil' somethin'"—Kendrick Lamar's "Fear"

E

eater
noun
1. a person who performs a lot of oral sex

EXAMPLE: "She a killer and an eater, she a Jeffrey Dahmer"—Juice Wrld's "Bandit" with YoungBoy Never Broke Again

F

facts

The truth or stating something, which people agree on

finna

about to, in the procces of
EXAMPLE: "I finna leave this motherfuckin place"

fire
adjective
1. something that's amazing, pleasant and attractive
2. weapons and ammo

EXAMPLE: "My head game is fire, punani Dasani/It's goin' in dry and it's comin' out soggy"—Cardi B's "WAP" with Megan Thee Stallion

fried

adjective
1. to be highly intoxicated

EXAMPLE: "In the function, and I'm fried, it's a strive, it's not a drive/When they open wide, it's a riot, riot"—Travis Scott's "No Bystanders" featuring Juice Wrld and Sheck Wes

flossin'
verb
1. showing off, stunting

EXAMPLE: "I don't need no one vouchin' for me/I be flossin', ain't talkin' 'bout my teeth"—Gunna's " Who You Foolin"

flex
verb
1. to boast about possessions or money

EXAMPLE: "Flexin' with a hunnid cash,"—Polo G's "Flex" featuring Juice Wrld

G

gas
adjective
1. high-grade marijuana
2. to hype someone

EXAMPLE: "I am smokin' on that gas, life should be on Cinemax/Movie "—2 Chainz's "No Lie" featuring Drake

glow up

A major improvement in one's self, usually an improvement in appearance, confidence, and style. Frequently used in a context relating to puberty.

goofy
noun
1. A lame, cornball

EXAMPLE: "I hate a goofy especially/They always dyin' to mention me"—Drake's "Hype"

H

hammer
noun
1. a gun

EXAMPLE: "Ayo, Eli, why they testin' me?/Like I don't always keep the hammer next to me"—Young M.A's "OOOUUU"

hard
noun
1. someone or something that is tough in manner

EXAMPLE: "I carved OF on it this morning with a glass shard/On my green mini ramp that I built in my backyard, that's hard"—Tyler, The Creator's "Colossus"

hits different

something that is better in a peculiar manner.

I

ice
noun
1. jewelry, diamonds

EXAMPLE: "Ice on my neck "—Lil Yachty on DRAM's "Broccoli"

irie
adjective
1. the state of feeling good
2. high, intoxicated

EXAMPLE: "I got dressed, I mixed the Tisa with Versace/I smoked a joint and took a bar, now I'm irie"—Ty Dolla $ign's "Irie" featuring Wiz Khalifa

Its giving...

Describe the attitude or connotation of something or someone.

J

jackin'
verb
1. not believing or thinking
2. stealing
3. claiming

EXAMPLE: "Now wildin', ready for all the violence/I don't need a n@$%# jacking that he riding"—6ix9ine's "Kika"

jabroni
noun
1. a lame, cornball

EXAMPLE: " I been with your mummy 'cause your daddy a jabroni"—Young Thug's "Jumped Out The Window"

K

knock
verb
1. to play loudly

EXAMPLE: "Tint the windows by the doors, let the four ride/Speakers knockin', they can hear me in the north side"—Mac Miller's "Special"

kiss
verb
1. to kill

EXAMPLE: "Jada, MWAH, I'll kiss you, you bitch-ass n@$%#/Bet the hood won't miss you, you bitch-ass n@$%#"—Jadakiss' "We Gonna Make It" featuring Styles P

L

Let him cook

Let one plan something

lick
noun
1. a way of making money
2. a drug fiend

EXAMPLE: "Bustin' all the bells out the box/I just hit a lick with the box"—Roddy Ricch's "The Box"

lit
adjective
1. something that's turned up
2. intoxicated

EXAMPLE: "30 for a walkthrough, man, we had that bitch lit/Had so many bottles, gave ugly girl a sip"—Post Malone's "Psycho" featuring Ty Dolla $ign

M

Mid

Of something to be average/mediocre

mop
noun
1. a firearm with a long clip

EXAMPLE: "I got the mop, watch me wash 'em like detergent/And I'm ballin', that's why it's diamonds on my jersey"—Roddy Ricch on DaBaby's "Rockstar"

moola
noun
1. money, currency

EXAMPLE: "She know I get that moola, man trappin' is a habit/We ballin' every night, baby, woah Kemosabe"—Future on Dej Loaf's "Hey There"

munch

A munch is someone who's only use is eating pussy without getting anything in return.

EXAMPLE: "Girl, I don't want him, he's just a munch"

N

Nina
noun
1. a handgun

EXAMPLE: "I bet a lot of n@$%#s plottin' so you know I got that heater, bruh/Drive my side of Harlem, catch me ridin' with my Nina, bruh"—A$AP Rocky's "Excuse Me"

nice
adjective
1. skilled

EXAMPLE: "Pull up on them bikes, let the throttle pop/N@$%#s know I'm nice, and I got a lot"—Meek Mill's "Flexing"

no cap
adverb
1. to tell the truth
2. no lie

EXAMPLE: "Opp, I'll slap the shit out a n@$%#/No talkin', I don't like to argue with n@$%#s (I don't)/Ain't gon' be no more laughin'/You see me whip out 'cause I'm gon' be done shot me a n@$%# (No cap)"—DaBaby's Suge

O

OD
adjective
1. past the limit
2. overdone

EXAMPLE: "Trips that you plan for the next whole week/Bands too long for a n@$%# so cheap/And your flex OD, and your sex OD"—Drake's "No Guidance" with Chris Brown

opp
noun
1. an enemy

EXAMPLE: "In New York I Milly Rock/Hide it in my sock/Running from an opp/And I shoot at opp"—Playboi Carti's "Magnolia"

Outta Pocket

Word used for when someone is out of line or acting up

Person: Dude that Danielle girl from Dr. Phil is just outta pocket,

You: That's what I'm sayin

P

P

noun
1. a positive thing

verb
1. player
2. keeping it real

EXAMPLE: "She let me squeeze, then she leave 'cause she keep it P"—Gunna and Future's "pushin P" featuring Young Thug

pack
noun
1. a dead person or thing
2. to carry a weapon
3. a collection of drugs

EXAMPLE: "My n@$%# sell crack like it's back in the '80s/Know a young n@$%#, he actin' so crazy/He serve a few packs and he jack a Mercedes/He shoot at the police, he clap at old ladies"—J. Cole's "KOD"

peon
noun
1. a soft, lame person

EXAMPLE: "These n@$%#s groupies, they peons, mane/King of my city like Leon, mane"—Lil Uzi Vert's "Lo Mein"

Periodt

Used to add emphasis to something

Q

quickie
noun
1. a brief sexual act
2. to do something in a hurry

EXAMPLE: "Yung Miami, yeah, bitch, I'm from the city/I'm litty, diamonds drippy, eat my pussy, that's a quickie"—Yung Miami on City Girls' "Twerkulator"

quarter
noun
1. one fourth of one million dollars
2. one fourth of an ounce in drugs

EXAMPLE: "Earrings cost a quarter, certified by GIA/If it's 'bout my bae or 'bout some smoke, I'm on my way"—21 Savage on Travis Scott's "NC-17"

R

rat
noun
1. a snitch

EXAMPLE: "Stuart Little, heard these n@$%#s some rats/Pockets full of cheese, bitch, I got racks"—21 Savage's "No Heart" with Metro Boomin

ratchet
adjective
1. out of pocket, unruly

EXAMPLE: "Not classy, I'm ratchet, if I twerk it, he gon' smack it/Put money in my basket, I got some expensive habits"—Flo Milli's "My Attitude"

Rizz

Rizz means you have game and get bitches

EXAMPLE: "Jonathan has rizz he gets mad play"

S

Shawty

A term used to describe an attractive young female.

EXAMPLE: "Yo shawty u wanna kick it at da club wit me?"

simp
noun
1. a desperate person, a person who does too much for someone they like

EXAMPLE: "Them whack hoes, y'all n@$%#s simpin'/Them bad hoes, my n@$%#s pimpin'"—Maxo Kream's "Hella Yellas"

slatt
phrase
1. slime love all the time

EXAMPLE: "In L.A., I smoke that gas/In L.A., I link with slatt"—Playboi Carti's "FlatBed Freestyle"

Slay

something to tell someone when they look gorgeous.

EXAMPLE: "omg slay"

slime
noun
1. a homie, ride or die
2. to do someone dirty

EXAMPLE: "She slid her hand down my pants just to grab the torpedo/I had to go back and link with my slimes like I'm 13 and zero"—Travis Scott on Young Thug's "Hot" with Gunna

straightenin'
verb
1. getting things right

EXAMPLE: "N@$%#s act like something been taken/Ain't nothing but a little bit of straightenin'"—Quavo on Migos' "Straightenin"

sucka
noun
1. a punk, chump

EXAMPLE: "I don't rap to suckas/God bless you all, I only talk special talk"—Jay-Z on DJ Khaled's "I Got The Keys" with Future

T

tech
noun
1. a semi-automatic pistol
2. lean, cough syrup

EXAMPLE: "Ayo, I walk through the valley of the shadow of death/Where n@$%#s hold techs like they mad at the ref"—J. Cole's "Forbidden Fruit"

thot or thotty
noun
1. an overindulgent person when it comes to sex

EXAMPLE: "I see two twin opps, leave 'em on a banner/And I got two thick thots, wanna link the gang, yeah"—Lil Tecca's "Ransom"

trippin

To act in a jestful or irrational manner.

To experience the affect of a mind-altering subtance, typically halucenogens.

EXAMPLE: "Why you trippin?"

U

up it
phrase
1. to raise weapons, shoot

EXAMPLE: "Hey, the beat go off?/I up it then my heat go off"—Chief Keef's "Earned It"

V

vamp
noun
1. someone who stays up all night
2. Playboi Carti's fan base

EXAMPLE: "When them vamps outside, lil' bitch, you better be ready/When them guns outside, lil' bitch, you better be ready"—Playboi Carti's "Vamp Anthem"

W

wetty
noun
1. an attractive woman
2. to be wet

EXAMPLE: "Fivio said she a wetty/I was sittin' at the trap house whippin' shit out the crocker like Betty"—Roddy Ricch's "Thailand"

WAP
phrase
1. an acronym for wet-ass pussy

EXAMPLE: "I'm talkin' WAP, WAP, WAP, that's some wet-ass pussy/Macaroni in a pot, that's some wet-ass pussy"—Cardi B's "WAP" with Megan Thee Stallion

Wallin

Used to describe a person/s who are **acting crazy**, **reckless**, **ridiculous**, etc.
-Pronounce: Wah-Lin
Dude 1: Yo what did your friends do at that party last night?

Dud 2: It was crazy! They destroyed everything!

Dude 1: Wow, your friends be wallin

X

Xanny
noun
1. Xanax

EXAMPLE: "She say I'm insane, yeah/I might blow my brain out/Xanny, help the pain, yeah/Please, Xanny, make it go away"—Lil Uzi Vert's "XO TOUR Llif3"

Y

yams
noun
1. a big butt

EXAMPLE: "I'm in the kitchen, yams everywhere/Just made a juug, I got bands everywhere"—2 Chainz's "Birthday Song"

YOLO
phrase
1. you only live once

EXAMPLE: "I'm screamin' out, 'YOLO,' yeah, that's still the motto/I know I be on some shit that they ain't thought of"—Lil Baby on Drake's "Wants and Needs"

Z

Zaza
noun
1. exotic, potent weed

EXAMPLE: "I smoke Zaza, I'm in La La off them trees/Took the T-tops off the 'Vette, I need a breeze"—Trippie Redd's "Weeeeee"

zooted
adjective
1. to be lit, highly intoxicated

EXAMPLE: "Popped me a Perc' and went ooh on her titties/Smokin' exotic, I'm zooted, I'm litty"—Lil Keed's "Tip Top"

This is a list of slang terminology used by Generation Z, or those born roughly between the late 1990s to the late 2000s in the Western world.

Generation Z slang differs significantly from slang terminology of prior generations in history in that Gen Z was the first generation to grow up entirely within the internet age. Due to this, much of their slang originates from online media such as social media apps like TikTok, YouTube, or Twitch. The ease of communication that comes with the internet also results in their slang being proliferated to a greater and swifter extent.

Much of Gen Z slang today was not termed by members of the generation itself but rather were terms already in use by certain communities. In many cases, Gen Z slang is derived from African-American vernacular English and LGBTQ+ slang. This has led to accusations of cultural appropriation

Members of the Gen Z years were born between 1997 and 2012. So as of 2023, the Gen Z age range is anywhere from 11 to 26. They are commonly referred to as the first fully "digitally native" generation. They grew up with social media and smartphones—they're used to living in a digital-first world.

What is Gen Z known for?

Characteristics of Generation Z

- They're money-driven and ambitious.
- They love to travel.
- They're prone to anxiety.
- They're known to set boundaries.
- They're avid gamers.
- They're nostalgic.
- They use social media in a unique way.

Generation Z favorite musical artists

- **Drake**
- **Eminem**
- **Taylor Swift**
- **Justin Bieber**
- **BTS**
- **Ariana Grande**

- Rihanna
- Kanye West
- Beyoncé
- Juice Wrld
- Lady Gaga
- NBA YoungBoy
- Lil Wayne
- Cardi B
- Lil Baby
- Nicki Minaj
- Michael Jackson
- Billie Eilish
- Chris Brown
- The Weekend
- Adele
- City Girls
- Lil Uzi Vert
- PlayBoi Carti
- Kid Cudi
- Tyler The Creator

The Basis of Gen Z Social Media

Gen Z is so obsessed with social media because it allows them to connect and build friendships with people all over the world. It's a powerful tool for building community and sharing information. And it's a great way to stay connected with friends and family. Unlike previous generations, Gen Z has little to no memory of a world without the internet, smartphones, and social media. Technology is a substantial part of their life. Being continually connected can also result in self-esteem issues and feeling pressure to conform.

Thank you for choosing this book, from this you will learn the basics of Gen-Z slang and what they like. Recommend this book to a friend to see their opinion.

Printed in Great Britain
by Amazon

52889091R00020